The Countries

Japan

Tamara L. Britton
ABDO Publishing Company

visit us at
www.abdopub.com

Published by ABDO Publishing Company, 4940 Viking Drive, Suite 622, Edina, Minnesota 55435. Copyright © 2000 Abdo Consulting Group, Inc., Pentagon Tower, P.O. Box 36036, Minneapolis, Minnesota 55435 USA. International copyrights reserved in all countries. No part of this book may be reproduced in any form without written permission from the publisher.

Published 2000
Printed in the United States of America
Second Printing 2002

Editors: Bob Italia, Kate A. Furlong
Art Direction & Maps: Patrick Laurel
Cover & Interior Design: MacLean & Tuminelly (Mpls.)
Interior Photos: Corbis, AP Photo Archive

Library of Congress Cataloging-in-Publication Data

Britton, Tamara L., 1963-
    Japan / Tamara L. Britton.
       p. cm. -- (The countries)
    Includes index.
    ISBN 1-57765-387-4
     1. Japan--Juvenile literature. I. Series.

DS806.B65 2000   00-033196

Contents

Kon-nichiwa!

Hello! Welcome to Japan. Japan is an ancient country in the Pacific Ocean. Japan is made up of islands. It has many volcanoes and earthquakes.

Japan was once an **aggressive** country. It conquered other nations. But after **World War II**, Japan had to give up its empire. Now, Japan is a peaceful, **democratic** nation.

Japan's high mountains and low beaches give it a varied climate. This makes Japan home to many different plants and animals. The world's largest **amphibian** and the only **canine** that **hibernates** live in Japan.

Almost all the people that live in Japan are Japanese. Some Chinese and Korean people live there, too. The Ainu are Japan's only native people.

Japan's people live in cities along the coastline at the base of the mountains. This makes Japan's cities very crowded. Students work hard and do well in school. They want to bring honor to their families.

But the Japanese people have fun, too. They celebrate many holidays. They watch sumo wrestling and baseball and play games. Japanese people like theater. *Noh* drama, *Kabuki*, and *Bunraku* are types of theater they enjoy.

Japan has had very prosperous times. But there have been difficult times, too. Japan is the only nation to have had a nuclear bomb dropped on it. But Japan's people have pulled together to make Japan a world **economic** power. Today, Japan is a wealthy, successful country.

A group of Japanese students say **kon-nichiwa!**

Fast Facts

OFFICIAL NAME: *Nippon* (Japan). In Japanese, *Nippon* means "land of the rising sun."

CAPITAL: Tokyo

LAND
- Highest Mountain Range: Japanese Alps
- Highest point: Mt. Fuji 12,388 feet (3,776 m)
- Lowest point: Lake Hachiro-gata 13 feet (4 m) below sea level
- Major Rivers: Shinano 228 miles (367 km) long
- Lakes: Biwa, Tazawa, Towada, Mashu

PEOPLE
- Population: 126,182,077 (1999 est.)
- Major Cities: Tokyo, Yokohama, Osaka, and Nagoya
- Language: Japanese
- Religion: Shinto and Buddhism

GOVERNMENT
- Form: Constitutional Monarchy
- Head: Prime Minister
- Legislature: Diet
- Flag: A red disk on a white field. The disk represents the sun.
- National Bird: Red-crowned Crane
- National Flower: Cherry Blossom
- National Anthem: "*Kimigayo*" ("The Reign of Our Emperor")
- Nationhood: Founded by Emperor Jimmu in 660 B.C.

ECONOMY
- Agricultural Products: Rice, sugar beets, vegetables, fruit, pork, poultry, dairy products, eggs, fish
- Mining Products: Iron, zinc, lead, gold, silver, copper
- Manufactured Products: Steel; electrical, construction and mining equipment; cars; electronic and telecommunications equipment; railroad equipment; ships; chemicals; textiles; processed foods
- Money: Yen

★ **Tokyo**

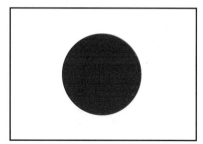

Japan's Flag

Japanese yen

Timeline

300 B.C.	Yamato clan unites Japan
A.D. 646	Taika reforms
1159	Heiji War
1192	Minamoto Yoritomo becomes *shogun*
1467	Onin War
1543	First Europeans come to Japan
1603	Tokugawa becomes *shogun*, moves capital to Edo
1853	Commodore Matthew C. Perry arrives in Japan
1854	Trade treaty signed
1868	Meiji Restoration, Edo renamed Tokyo
1910	Japan annexes Korea
1926	Hirohito becomes emperor
1931	Japan conquers Manchuria
1937	Japan goes to war with China
1940	Japan signs Tripartite Pact
1941	Japan attacks Pearl Harbor
1945	U.S. drops atomic bombs on Japan, Japan surrenders
1951	Japan signs peace treaty
1989	Hirohito dies, Akihito becomes emperor
1980s	Rapid economic expansion
1990s	Economic uncertainty

Clans and Emperors

Japan's first settlers crossed the Sea of Japan from Asia. They founded small villages and began farming. They practiced the **Shinto** religion and lived in **clans** called *uji*. Each clan had its own gods and leaders.

In about 300 B.C., the Yamato clan began to unite Japan's settlers. In A.D. 646, the Taika **reforms** made the Yamato clan ruler Japan's emperor. Yamato family members have been Japan's emperors ever since.

The Taika reforms also forbid large landholdings and gave some of the land to peasants. Taxes were soon collected. To encourage agriculture, tax breaks were given to people who farmed new land.

This created large farms called *shoen*. Clans owned the *shoen*.

The Heiji War

But peasants worked the land. Warriors called samurai protected the clan and its *shoen*.

Clans with large *shoen* and many samurai fought for power. The most powerful clan controlled Japan. In

1159, the Minamoto and Taira clans fought the Heiji War. The Taira won and ruled Japan for awhile. But the Minamoto rebelled and took power in 1185.

In 1192, Minamoto Yoritomo became *shogun*, or chief military commander. A 1333 revolt against Minamoto led to the Onin War of 1467. Fighting between **clans** for power caused civil wars in Japan until the late 1500s.

Minamoto Yoritomo

During this time, Japan began **foreign** trade. Japanese traders sailed to China and Korea. In 1543, the first European traders came to Japan. Soon, Christian **missionaries** arrived. They began to convert the Japanese to Christianity.

In the 1560s, Oda Nobunaga started to unite Japan's clans. He died in 1582, and Toyotomi Hideyoshi took his place. Toyotomi led invasions of Korea in an attempt to conquer China. He died in 1598. Tokugawa Ieyasu replaced him. Tokugawa moved the capital to Edo and became *shogun* in 1603.

Tokugawa feared foreigners might conquer Japan. So, Christian missionaries were expelled. Christianity was forbidden. Foreign trade ended. And Japan's people could not leave the country. This period of **seclusion** lasted more than 200 years.

In 1853, Commodore Matthew C. Perry arrived from the U.S. He wanted to make a treaty so the U.S. and Japan could trade. Japan feared U.S. military power, so it signed the treaty in 1854. Soon, other countries came to trade with Japan.

Commodore Matthew C. Perry

Most Japanese did not like opening their country to **foreigners**. Many people wanted Tokugawa to quit. They wanted the emperor to rule Japan. So, in 1868, Emperor Mutsuhito took control of the government and forced the Tokugawa **clan** out of power. The shift in power from clan leaders to the emperor is called the Meiji Restoration.

Emperor Mutsuhito

A central government was established, and Edo was renamed Tokyo. Social classes ended. An army was created to replace the samurai warriors.

The government created modern money and banking systems. It built railroads, factories, and telephone and telegraph lines. In 1889, a **constitution** went into effect.

Emperor Hirohito

The emperor was afraid of Western power. So, Japan set out to build its own empire. After wars with Russia and China, Japan gained control of Taiwan and some Russian land. In 1910, Japan **annexed** Korea. Five years later, Japan gained power in the Manchuria region in China. Japan had become a world power.

In 1912, Emperor Mutsuhito died. His son Yoshihito became emperor. But Yoshihito became ill, and in 1926, his son Hirohito became emperor. During the 1920s, Japan's military gained power. In 1931, Japan conquered Manchuria.

In 1936, events leading to **World War II** began in Europe. In 1937, Japan went to war against China.

In 1940, Japan signed the Tripartite Pact with **Axis** countries Germany and Italy. Japan also sent troops to occupy Indochina. The U.S. used **economic sanctions** to try to stop Japan's **aggressive** behavior. But the sanctions did not work.

Japanese troops enter Manchuria.

On December 7, 1941, Japan bombed the U.S. naval base at Pearl Harbor, Hawaii. Japan hoped to expand its empire by crippling U.S. naval power in the Pacific. It also hoped to discourage America and the **Allies** from entering into a long, expensive war with them.

Instead, the U.S. quickly **declared** war against Japan and the other **Axis** countries. On April 19, 1942, the U.S. Army bombed Tokyo and defeated Japan in the Midway Islands. But Japan would not give up.

On May 8, 1945, Germany **surrendered** and the Allies won the war in Europe. This is called V-E Day. But Japan still would not give up.

On August 6, 1945, the U.S. dropped an atomic bomb on the Japanese city of Hiroshima. Still, Japan kept fighting. So, on August 9, the U.S. dropped another atomic bomb on Nagasaki.

Japan finally surrendered on September 2, 1945. This is called V-J Day.

An Allied journalist stands in Hiroshima after the bombing. The building in the background is now a memorial.

The U.S. occupied Japan after the war. Japan's army was broken up. Now, Japan could only have a small army for self-defense. This stopped Japan from waging future wars.

A new **constitution** was written in 1947. It made Japan a **democracy**. On September 8, 1951, Japan signed a peace treaty with 47 other nations. The U.S. occupation ended when the treaty went into effect on April 28, 1952.

After **World War II**, Japan rebuilt its **economy** by working and studying hard. During this time, the rest of Asia was destroyed by war. And China was turning to **communism**. This helped make Japan's economy successful.

Emperor Akihito

In 1989, Emperor Hirohito died. He was Japan's longest-reigning leader. His son Akihito became emperor.

Today, Japan faces uncertainty. Overspending in the 1980s weakened its economy. Many businesses have failed. Japan's position as an economic power is threatened.

But Japan's people continue to work and study hard. Their strong spirit and national pride will help them through difficult times to new success, as it has throughout their long history.

Land of the Rising Sun

Japan is an island nation. The Pacific Ocean borders Japan on the north and east. The East China Sea lies to Japan's south. The Sea of Japan lies to the east, separating Japan from the Asian coast.

Japan's four main islands are Hokkaido, Honshu, Shikoku, and Kyushu. Japan also has almost 4,000 smaller islands.

Japan is located near three major plates of the Earth's crust. The Pacific and the Philippine plates are sinking under the Eurasian Plate. This movement causes earthquakes in Japan.

Japan has about 1,000 earthquakes every year. Some are more than 7 on the **Richter scale**. Earthquakes happen under the sea, too. These earthquakes cause *tsunamis*. These giant waves slam into Japan's Pacific coast, causing major flooding.

The plate movement has formed many mountains in Japan. Mountains form a ridge down the nation's center. **Fertile** plains can be found between the mountain ridges and between the mountains and the seas.

Mt. Fuji

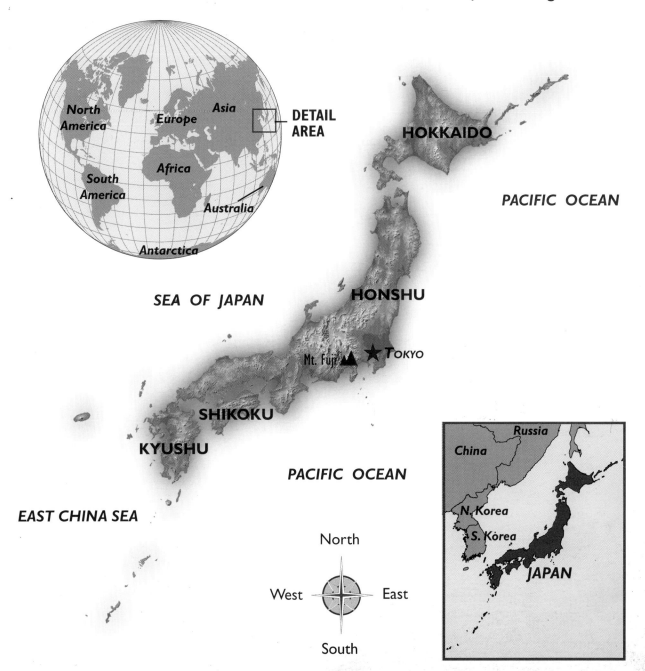

DETAIL AREA

North America

Europe

Asia

Africa

South America

Australia

Antarctica

HOKKAIDO

PACIFIC OCEAN

SEA OF JAPAN

HONSHU

Mt. Fuji ▲▲ ★ TOKYO

SHIKOKU

KYUSHU

PACIFIC OCEAN

EAST CHINA SEA

North

West   East

South

Russia

China

N. Korea

S. Korea

JAPAN

Japan's short rivers run down the mountains to the sea. They are not good for navigation. But they are used for irrigation and **hydro-electric** power.

Japan is also located along the **Ring of Fire**. Japan has almost 300 volcanoes. The highest is Mt. Fuji, which is **dormant**. Volcanoes formed many of Japan's lakes. Some lakes, such as Towada, are in **calderas**. Others, such as the Five Fuji Lakes, were formed when lava dammed rivers.

Japan stretches about 1,500 miles (2,414 km) from north to south. Because of its length and different elevations, Japan has many climates. The north has warm summers and long, cold winters with lots of snow. Central Japan has hot summers and short winters. And southern Japan has long, hot, humid summers and short winters.

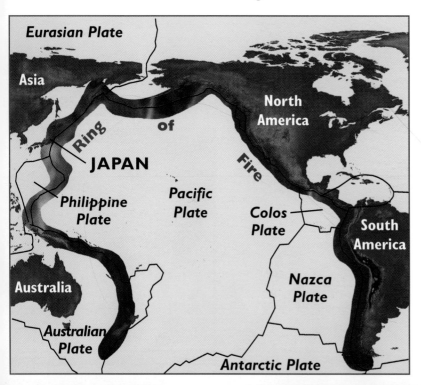

The Ring of Fire

Rainfall

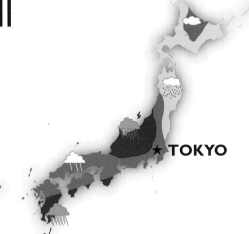

AVERAGE YEARLY RAINFALL

Inches		Centimeters
Over 80		Over 200
60 - 80		150 - 200
40 - 60		100 - 150
20 - 40		50 - 100

★ TOKYO

Temperature

Winter

Summer

AVERAGE TEMPERATURE

Fahrenheit		Celsius
68° - 86°		20° - 30°
50° - 68°		10° - 20°
32° - 50°		0° - 10°
14° - 32°		-10° - 0°
Under -4°		Under -20°

★ TOKYO

Wild Things

Japan's varied land and climate make it home to many plants and animals. In the north, spruce and fir trees grow with birch, oak, and maple.

In the north's highest mountains, shrubs and creeping pine grow. These mountains are home to brown bears, Asian black bears, wild boars, and foxes.

The raccoon dog, *tanuki*, also lives in this region. The *tanuki* looks like a raccoon. It has short legs, a heavy body, and rounded ears. It is the only **canine** that **hibernates**. In Japanese folklore, *tanukis* are mischievous animals that are always in trouble.

Japanese macaques live on the northern tip of Honshu. This is the most northern **habitat** for any monkey in the world. Macaques are losing their home as people cut down forests for lumber. But some groups are working to save the macaque's habitat.

Japanese macaques

Mangrove trees

Western Honshu and Kyushu are home to Japanese giant salamanders. They are the world's largest **amphibian**. They can grow to 4 feet (1 m) or more and weigh 80 pounds (36 kg). They have smooth, moist skin instead of scales. They live in the water but come to the surface to breathe.

Central and southern Japan have camphor, pasania, Japanese evergreen, and oak trees. Ficus and palm trees also grow in the south. Kyushu's southern coast has mangrove swamps. The Rykukyu and Bonin Islands have semi-tropical rainforests with mulberry, camphor, and oak trees.

Many kinds of birds live near Japan's coasts. Ducks, swans, herons, and white-tailed eagles nest there. The red-crowned crane, Japan's national bird, lives in Hokkaido's wetlands. It is the world's largest crane. Hunters have killed many of them. Today, it is against the law to kill the red-crowned crane.

The red-crowned crane

Japan's People

Most people in Japan are Japanese. They follow the **Shinto** and **Buddhist** religions. Japan's minority groups are Koreans, Chinese, and Ainu people.

The Ainu are Japan's only native people. As Japan's population increased, they were pushed from their lands. Today, the Ainu are organizing to fight for the same rights that other Japanese people have.

An Ainu family

Street signs in Tokyo are read from top to bottom.

Most people in Japan speak Japanese. Japanese is read from top to bottom, instead of from left to right like English.

Japanese is written three ways. *Kanji* is written with Chinese symbols. Each symbol stands for a word. *Hiragana* symbols are used when there is no *Kanji* symbol for a word. There are thousands of *Kanji* and *Hiragana* symbols. *Katakana* is used to write words that came from Western languages.

Sometimes people who do not know how to write Japanese need to write Japanese words. When people write Japanese words in English, the Japanese call the words *romanji*.

Japanese students begin learning *kanji* symbols in elementary school. Japanese kids must go to school from age 6 to age 15. First they go to one to three years of kindergarten. Next, they go to lower school. Kids who want to continue their schooling go to upper secondary school. Nearly all students go on.

Education in Japan is very competitive. Students work hard to get good grades. They want to go to good colleges. Students who graduate from the top universities get the best jobs in business and government.

To make sure they can pass college entrance tests, some students go to *juku*, or cram school. Students go to *juku* for three hours after regular school. *Juku* study begins in nursery school and goes through secondary school.

Poor performance in school is a bad reflection on a student and his or her family. So, most

A Japanese student learns to write.

students in Japan always go to school and study hard. They want to bring honor and pride to their families.

A Japanese building with tatami mats and sliding paper walls

Japanese families live in many types of houses. People who live in crowded cities live in big apartment buildings. But some still live in **traditional** Japanese wooden houses. These houses have paper walls that slide to make rooms bigger or smaller.

In Japanese houses, *tatami* mats cover the floor. People must take off their shoes before going in the house. People sit on large pillows instead of chairs, and they sleep on large cushions called futons.

Today, most Japanese people wear Western-style clothes such as business suits, dresses, and blue jeans. Most children wear uniforms to school. But on special occasions, they wear traditional *hakama* pants, *haori* shirts, and *kimonos*.

Japanese families begin the day with a breakfast of rice, eggs, miso soup, fish, seaweed, and vegetables. They eat with chopsticks. Japanese children begin learning to use chopsticks when they are very young. Lunch is often noodles, rice with vegetables, or a sandwich. Students bring lunch to school in a *bento* box. Vendors also sell *bento* box lunches. Dinner is the day's main meal. Rice, soup, fish, and vegetables are served.

Donburi

Rice is Japan's most important crop. Rice is eaten at every meal in Japan. Rice is so important in the Japanese diet, the word for breakfast, *asa-gohan*, means "morning rice." The word for lunch, *hiru-gohan*, means "noon rice," and dinner, *yuu-gohan*, means "evening rice."

Donburi is a popular meal. To make *Donburi*, fill a bowl with cooked rice. Then, put cooked meat, vegetables, or eggs on top. Delicious!

AN IMPORTANT NOTE TO THE CHEF: Always have an adult help with the preparation and cooking of food. Never use kitchen utensils or appliances without adult permission and supervision.

Money Matters

After **World War II**, Japan worked hard to rebuild and regain its position as a world leader. Now, Japan has the second-largest **economy** in the world, after the United States. It also has the highest **cost of living**.

Japan's land makes agriculture a challenge. Only a small amount of land is available for farming. And the soil requires fertilizer and careful attention to grow good crops.

But Japan's farmers can grow more than half of the food that Japan's people need. The most valuable crop is rice. Japan also grows wheat, barley, potatoes, tea, cabbages, sugarcane, and sugar beets. Other farm products are fruit, cattle, and dairy products.

Japan has the largest fishing fleet in the world. It catches more tuna than any other country. The fleet also brings in sardines, cod, herring, salmon, and seaweed. Japan catches more fish than any other

A farmer tends his rice field. Rice is grown on more than half of Japan's farmland.

Fishermen sort the day's catch.

nation. Because Japan catches so many fish, other countries have claimed **economic** zones in their coastal waters. This limits the amount of fish **foreign** countries can catch near their borders. This assures that there will be plenty of fish for everyone.

Manufacturing is also important in Japan's economy. Japan makes more than 11 million motor **vehicles** a year. Japan also makes steel, ships, and electronic equipment.

Mining makes up the smallest part of Japan's economy. Japan mines coal, iron, zinc, lead, copper, gold, and silver. Japan's iron is poor quality, so the iron needed to make steel is mostly **imported**. Copper was once Japan's most important ore, but the supply is almost gone. Now, Japan imports most of its copper, too.

Workers build cars at this factory in Quito. Cars are Japan's chief export.

Splendid Cities

Tokyo is Japan's largest city. Tokyo means "eastern capital." About ten million people live there. It is on Honshu's Pacific coast, at the head of Tokyo Bay.

Tokyo is Japan's business center. Many Japanese and **foreign** businesses have their headquarters there. Products from all over the world are distributed from Tokyo Bay. Many **exports** leave Japan from there, too. The world's biggest fish market is in Tokyo. Tsukiji market sells more than 2,500 tons (2,540 t) of fish every day.

Tokyo is also Japan's cultural center. The Imperial Palace is in Tokyo. This is where the emperor lives. The Tokyo National Museum is in Ueno Park. It also has a zoo, science museum, and two art museums. There are theaters in Tokyo for *Kabuki* and *Noh* drama, as well as opera and symphony orchestras. Tokyo University is one of the best in Japan.

The Imperial Palace

Tokyo, Japan

Yokohama is Japan's second largest city. Around four million people live there. It is about 20 miles (32 km) southwest of Tokyo. These two cities form the Tokyo-Yokohama Metropolitan Area.

Yokohama was established in 1889. The Great Kanto Earthquake destroyed it in 1923. In 1945, bombs in **World War II** damaged it. But Yokohama was rebuilt and has become an important port city.

Much of Japan's heavy industry is in Yokohama. People build ships, produce chemicals, machinery, petroleum products, cars, and metal products.

Yokohama's Sankei Garden contains many historic buildings. Nogeyama Park has an open-air theater, a concert hall, and a zoo. Yokohama has four universities. It also has the Kanazawa Library, which is famous for its collection of historical books.

Yokohama's large port imports most of the materials needed for manufacturing and industry.

Japan on the Move

Japan has one of the world's most developed transportation systems. Railways, roads, and airports connect Japan's islands.

The railway system in Japan has streetcars, subways, and trains. Every day, hundreds of people ride trains called *Shinkansen*, or bullet trains. These high-speed trains can go faster than 180 mph (290 k/h)! The *Shinkansen* get crowded during rush hour. People called pushers are used to push as many people onto a train as will fit.

Japan **exports** many cars and trucks each year. But many stay home, too. Today, lots of Japanese families own two or more cars.

Highways have been built between major cities. There are expressways within large metropolitan areas. But Japan's road network is small compared to the number of cars that use it. There is not enough room to build needed roads.

A Shinkansen *train speeds past Mt. Fuji.*

Bridges and undersea tunnels connect Japan's four major islands. Trains, cars, and trucks can travel on the bridges and in the tunnels. Japan has the world's longest undersea tunnel. The Seikan Tunnel connects Honshu and Hokkaido across the Tsugaru Strait. It is 33.4 miles (53.8 km) long, and took 24 years to build!

Busy highways in Tokyo

Many airports serve Japan. **Foreign** flights use New Tokyo International Airport, called Narita Airport. Haneda Airport is also near Tokyo. The Kansai International Airport is in Osaka. It was built on a man-made island in Osaka Bay! Japan Airlines and All Nippon Airlines are the country's two national airlines.

Japan has many ways to transport its goods and people. But so many trains, cars, and airplanes in such a small area have created air pollution. To help keep things moving and to keep the air clean, Japan has created strict **emissions** standards for cars and trucks. It has also built noise barriers in populated areas.

Japan's Government

Japan's government is a **constitutional monarchy**. The constitution divides Japan's government into three branches. They are the executive, judicial, and legislative.

Japan's emperor has a mostly ceremonial role. He presides over national ceremonies, presents awards, and calls the legislature to order at the beginning of each session.

The prime minister is chosen by the legislature and appointed by the emperor. The prime minister appoints a cabinet that holds executive power and supervises the government's departments.

Japan's legislative branch is called the Diet. It is made up of the House of Councillors and the House of Representatives. Voters elect the members of both houses.

The government's judicial branch is made up of five courts. The highest one is called the Supreme Court. It has a chief justice as well as 14 other justices. The chief justice is selected by the cabinet and appointed by the emperor.

Locally, Japan is divided in 47 prefectures. Prefectures are big cities with more than a million citizens. Voters of each prefecture elect a governor. They also elect representatives to sit on the prefecture's assembly.

The next level of government is the municipality. Municipalities are towns and villages. Japan has 3,000 municipalities. Each municipality's citizens elect a mayor and a municipal assembly.

Japan's government is working to make Japan a good place for its citizens. But some Japanese are upset about the 1947 **Constitution**. They miss the old ways. Others support Japan's new government. They feel that **democracy** gives the Japanese people more opportunities and protects their political freedom and **civil rights**.

U.S. president Bill Clinton speaks at a meeting of the Diet.

Holidays & Festivals

In Japan, people work and study very hard. But it is not all work and no play! Japanese people celebrate many holidays and festivals throughout the year.

Shogatsu is the biggest holiday in Japan. It is a celebration of the New Year. Japanese people clean their homes and businesses to get a fresh start on the new year. Some people wear traditional Japanese clothing and families get together to have a big meal. Temples ring their bells at midnight on New Year's Eve. *Shogatsu* festivities last several days.

An important holiday for young people is Coming-of-Age Day on January 15. After this day, all 20-year-old Japanese are adults. They can vote, get

Cherry trees in bloom

married, and make decisions without their parent's permission. To celebrate, the young men and women march in a parade and have parties. They also get presents from their friends and families.

Setsubun, or the Bean-throwing Festival, marks the end of winter. Priests from the temples throw beans into the crowds. People chant a verse to bring good luck and ward off evil spirits. In Hokkaido, there is a Snow Festival in February.

In the summer, people like to go on vacation during Golden Week. Golden Week is from April 29 through May 5. During this time, the cherry trees bloom. People visit parks and have picnics under the trees to enjoy the beautiful pink flowers.

In July or August, the Bon Celebration honors dead ancestors. Festival participants float lanterns lit with candles on water. In November, during the *Shichi-go-san* Festival, children dress up and visit their favorite shrines. There, they pray for health and good luck.

A young Japanese girl wears a **kimono** *at a* **Shichi-go-san** *Festival.*

Sports & Leisure

Japanese people enjoy many different sports. Sumo wrestling is Japan's national sport. Sumo wrestlers weigh more than 300 pounds (136 kg)! They live with a sumo master and have strict training. They compete in six tournaments a year. Only a few wrestlers achieve the highest rank of *yokozuna*, or grand champion.

Baseball is also popular in Japan. The first professional league was formed in 1936. Today, there are two leagues. The Central and Pacific leagues compete each year in the Japan Series to determine the best team in Japan.

Japanese also like to play games. Two popular games are Go and *pachinko*. Go is a game that resembles checkers and chess. Each player tries to surround the other player's game pieces with his own. The player that surrounds most of the opposing player's pieces wins. *Pachinko* is a type of pinball game. *Pachinko* is the sound the ball makes when the player shoots it into the game!

Sumo wrestling

A Japanese man plays **pachinko.**

Karaoke started in Japan in the 1970s. In Japanese, *karaoke* means empty orchestra. *Karaoke* is a music tape with no voice on it. A person can sing along with the tape. Today, *karaoke* is popular all over the world.

Many Japanese listen to pop music sung by *idoru kashus*, or singing idols. But many also like music played on traditional Japanese instruments. The *koto* is a flat instrument with thirteen strings. A *samisen* is like a banjo, but it only has three strings. A *shakuhachi* is a flute made from bamboo. *Taiko* are drums.

Some Japanese make art from paper. Origami is the art of folding paper into patterns that make birds, fish, kites, hats, and masks. Children learn origami in school.

Japanese musicians play traditional instruments. They are (l to r), a koto, another koto, a samisen, and a shakuhachi.

A man carrying a bonsai

Many Japanese practice the ancient art of Bonsai. Bonsai are miniature trees that are shaped to look like regular-sized trees. Bonsai are planted in small containers. It takes many years to shape a bonsai tree. Some bonsai are passed down through families.

Japanese like to attend theater. *Noh* drama are serious plays that were once performed for an upper-class audience. They combine music, dance, acting, and poetry. *Kabuki* plays were for working-class people. They portray scenes from everyday life.

Bunraku is puppet theater. *Bunraku* puppets are not hand puppets. They are big puppets operated with strings. Sometimes it takes many people to operate a *Bunraku* puppet!

A Kabuki *play*

Today, Japanese people can enjoy many leisure activities. They have risen above the difficult time after **World War II** to become an **economic** power. Japan's people are changing as more opportunities become available and fewer people follow **traditional** ways. But the Japanese people have a unique culture and history that binds them into a strong nation that will continue to flourish.

*In **Bunraku** puppet shows, some of the puppet operators dress in black so they are not noticeable.*

Glossary

aggressive - displaying hostile actions.

allies - countries that help each other in times of need. During World War II, Great Britain, France, the U.S., and the Soviet Union were called the Allies.

amphibians - cold-blooded animals with backbones that have characteristics between a fish and a reptile.

annex - to add land to a nation.

axis - during World War II, Germany, Italy, and Japan were called the Axis Powers.

Buddhism - a religion that was started in India by Buddha. It teaches that pain and evil are caused by desire. If people have no desire they will achieve a state of happiness called nirvana.

caldera - the crater of a volcano.

canine - a member of the dog family.

civil rights - the individual rights of a citizen, such as the right to vote or freedom of speech.

clan - a group of families in a community that descended from a common ancestor.

communism - an economic system in which everything is owned by the government and given to the people as they need it.

constitution - a paper that describes a country's laws and government.

cost of living - the average cost of goods and services. In countries with a high cost of living, goods and services are expensive.

declare - to make a public, formal announcement.

democracy - a governmental system in which the citizens vote on how to run the country.

dormant - not active.

economy - the way a country uses its money, goods, and natural resources.

emissions - harmful gasses that are released with a vehicle's exhaust.

export - to send goods to another country to sell or trade.

fertile - land that is able to produce plentiful crops.

foreign - from another country.

habitat - the area where a plant or animal naturally lives.

hibernate - to spend the winter in an inactive state.

hydro-electric - electricity produced by water-powered generators.

import - to bring in goods from another country to sell or trade.

missionary - a person sent by a church to spread the church's religion to people who do not believe it.

monarchy - a government controlled by a king or queen.

reform - to make something better by getting rid of its faults.

Richter scale - a scale for measuring the strength of earthquakes invented by Charles F. Richter. The scale goes from 1, which is a small earthquake, to 10, which is a very harmful earthquake.

Ring of Fire - a nearly continuous chain of volcanoes that surrounds the Pacific Ocean.

sanctions - measures by several nations against a nation that has violated international law. Sanctions are meant to force the offending nation to comply with the law.

seclusion - being apart or cut off from others.

Shinto - the native religion of Japan. Shinto is marked by worship of nature, respect of ancestors and ancient heroes, and the divinity of the emperor.

surrender - to give up.

tradition - something that has been passed down through generations.

vehicle - a mechanical device powered by an engine used for transporting people and goods. Cars, trucks, heavy equipment, and buses are types of vehicles.

World War II - 1939 to 1945, fought in Europe, Asia, and Africa. The U.S., France, Great Britain, the Soviet Union, and their allies fought Germany, Italy, Japan, and their allies. The war began when Germany invaded Poland. It ended when Japan surrendered after the U.S. bombed Nagasaki and Hiroshima.

English	Japanese
Yes	Hai
No	Iie
Thank You	Ari Gato
Please	Douzo
Hello	Kon-nichiwa
Goodbye	Sayounara
Mother	Okansan
Father	Otousan

Web Sites

Japan: A Country Study
http://lcweb2.loc.gov/frd/cs/jptoc.html
The Library of Congress sponsors this site on Japan. It has exhaustive information on Japan's history, society, economy, government and politics, and military.

CIA: The World Factbook - 1999
http://www.odci.gov/cia/publications/factbook/
This site by the CIA offers up-to-date statistics on Japan. It has sections on Japan's geography, people, government, economy, communications, transportation, and military.

These sites are subject to change. Go to your favorite search engine and type in "Japan" for more sites.

Index